DIY HACKS
De-clutter Your Home In 7 Days!

2nd Edition

By Sally Lemon

© **Copyright 2015 by Sally Lemon - All rights reserved.**

In no way is it legal to reproduce, duplicate, or transmit any part of this document in either electronic means or in printed format. Recording of this publication is strictly prohibited and any storage of this document is not allowed unless with written permission from the publisher. All rights reserved.

The information provided herein is stated to be truthful and consistent, in that any liability, in terms of inattention or otherwise, by any usage or abuse of any policies, processes, or directions contained within is the solitary and utter responsibility of the recipient reader. Under no circumstances will any legal responsibility or blame be held against the publisher for any reparation, damages, or monetary loss due to the information herein, either directly or indirectly.

Respective authors own all copyrights not held by the publisher.

Legal Notice:

This book is copyright protected. This is only for personal use. You cannot amend, distribute, sell, use, quote or paraphrase any part or the content within this book without the consent of the author or copyright owner. Legal action will be pursued if this is breached.

Disclaimer Notice:

Please note the information contained within this document is for educational and entertainment purposes only. Every attempt has been made to provide accurate, up to date and reliable complete information. No warranties of any kind are expressed or implied. Readers acknowledge that the author is not engaging in the rendering of legal, financial, medical or professional advice.

By reading this document, the reader agrees that under no circumstances are we responsible for any losses, direct or indirect, which are incurred as a result of the use of information contained within this document, including, but not limited to, —errors, omissions, or inaccuracies.

Contents

INTRODUCTION

CHAPTER 1: DO YOU HAVE CLUTTER?

    WHY DO YOU WANT AN ORGANIZED HOME?
    TRY TO IDENTIFY YOUR BIG PICTURE
    REASONS WHY YOU NEED TO DECLUTTER!
        Reason 1 – Control your need for buying and storing
        Reason 2 – You should own your possessions
        Reason 3 – You need to live an uncluttered life
    WHAT IF YOU HAD AN ORGANIZED LIFE?

CHAPTER 2: THE PSYCHOLOGY OF CLUTTERING

    MOVE OUT OF YOUR TRANCE
        Exercise
    HOW DO YOUR SHAKE OUT OF YOUR TRANCE?
        How to Avoid Purchasing unnecessary stuff?

CHAPTER 3: DEFINING CLUTTER!

    THE THREE TYPES OF CLUTTER
        Inner Clutter
        Outer Clutter
        Other Clutter
    HOW THE TYPES OF CLUTTER AFFECT YOU
    THE NEED FOR FOCUS
    WHY ARE YOU GOING TO TRY ORGANIZING YOUR CLUTTER?
        Yourself
        Family
        Children
        Successors

CHAPTER 4: WHY DO WE HAVE INNER CLUTTER?

    LAYERS OF PROBLEMS CAUSE CLUTTER
    FOCUS

Self – inquiry for inner decluttering
Why do we have clutter?

CHAPTER 5: PROJECT DECLUTTER!

What are the reasons for cluttering?
The two important steps to organize clutter
Decide
Action
How to keep yourself motivated while decluttering?
Give yourself deadlines
Create a declutter Buddy system

CHAPTER 6: MATERIALS TO MAKE YOU FASTER AND MORE EFFECTIVE

Mop
Windex
All-purpose cleaner
Baking Soda
Microfiber wipes
Gloves
Polish

CHAPTER 7: THE FENG SHUI AND DECLUTTERING

What is Feng Shui?
How do you use Feng Shui for your house?
Feng Shui tips
Seating, Shapes and the Spatial Relations
Windows, the Colors and the organized Clutter
Décor

CHAPTER 8: MONDAY - GETTING RID OF THE DUSTS

Electronics
Furniture and curio cabinets

- CARPET, RUGS, SOFT TOYS
- IN HIDDEN AREAS
- VENTS
- CEILING FANS

CHAPTER 9: TUESDAY - CLEANING THE BATHROOM

- CLEAN WASHROOM CURTAINS AND MATS FIRST
- DIRT FREE YOUR SHOWER
- CLEANING OF TILES, WALLS AND CEILING
- CLEANING SINK AND BATH-TUB
- TOILET CLEANING

CHAPTER 10: WEDNESDAY - CLEANING THE KITCHEN

- GET YOUR CLEANING SPONGES READY
- FOLLOW INSTRUCTION MANUAL TO CLEAN APPLIANCES
- CLEANING COOK-TOP
- CLEANING THE COUNTER TOP
- CLEANING THE FLOOR

CHAPTER 11: THURSDAY - CLEANING THE BEDROOMS

- TAKE OUT ALL THE FURNISHINGS AND CLEAN THEM OUT
- CLEANING CABINETS AND REORGANIZING THEM
- CLEAN AND POLISH BEDROOM FURNITURE
- ADD THE TINGE OF YOUR FAVORITE AROMA IN YOUR BEDROOM
- TIPS TO MAKE BEDROOM CLEANING FUN
- FENG SHUI TIPS FOR YOUR BEDROOM

CHAPTER 12: FRIDAY - CLEANING THE LIVING ROOM

- DUSTING AND CLEANING OF FURNISHING AND UPHOLSTERIES
- WINDOW CLEANING
- CLEANING OF FIXTURES

- Vacuum clean drapes, blinds and sofas
- Dust and clean your souvenirs
- Cleaning of your indoor plants
- Things to take care of while sanitizing your living room
- Feng Shui tips for your living room

CHAPTER 13: SATURDAY - CLEANING THE FLOORS

- Cleaning of wood floors
- Tiled/Marble floors cleaning
- Cleaning of ceramic floors
- Cleaning of vinyl floor
- Cleaning of brick floors

CHAPTER 14: SUNDAY - FAMILY BONDING WHILE ORGANIZING

- Divide jobs of cleaning
- Do not force it on people
- Make it a fun task
- Catch up with an old friend on phone while cleaning alone
- Treat your family members on the last day of cleaning

CHAPTER 15: THE RULES TO REMEMBER WHEN YOU ARE DECLUTTERING

CONCLUSION

Introduction

Thank you for purchasing the book, *DIY HACKS: De-clutter Your Home In 7 Days!*

Cleanliness is an essential part of our overall wellness drive and home cleaning is an integral part of complete cleaning process. Keeping our home clean not only endows us with a healthy life but it also puts positive impact on our psychology. It has been observed that people who live in a clean and fragrant atmosphere enjoy better mood stability than those who pay least attention towards hygiene and sanitization.

The book helps you identify the different reasons why you have clutter at home. You may love shopping with all your heart. But soon that shopping is going to bring the condition of your house down. You have to know that the clutter that you own will eventually kill you. You will have to know that clutter is like a gun. It does not kill you. It is you who kill yourself. Your clutter may turn you crazy at times. You may wish for a natural calamity. You have to realize this sooner than later.

The book provides you with the psychological aspect of clutter. Psychologists believe that people are in a trance when they have to go shopping. They go with a certain idea in their head but then they end up doing something entirely different. This is because they are hypnotized. The book provides you with different techniques that you can use to get out of the trance.

But then you have the next question. How do you clean your

house? How will you work on removing all the clutter that you have at home? Although, there are many professional service providers who offer home-cleaning services you should have thought of cleaning your house on your own. It will help you in staying under your budget as well as will prove to be a fun task.

This book provides you with a schedule that will help you begin your decluttering process. This schedule is a blue print. You can work around it and make sure that you organize your house within a week! Scroll down and know how you can turn the home-cleaning act into a happy family-bonding event. Try to make use of your holiday season. Start from Monday and step into a cleaner habitat on the coming Sunday. This week long event is designed in step-wise cleaning schedule that helps you to keep your house dirt free in a hassle-free manner.

Thank you for purchasing the book. I hope it helps you!

Chapter 1: Do You Have Clutter?

There are numerous TV shows that talk exclusively about clutter. There are radio shows that love it! They have phone-ins where you ask questions about clutter and how you can get rid of it. There are numerous articles in magazines that tell you about it. Did you know there is a billion dollar industry that actually helps you keep yourself and your clutter organized? You may have come across numerous blogs, newsletters, forums and even classes on how you must control yourself from splashing your money out on objects that you want to squeeze into every corner in your house. There are people who actually love doing this. You can hire them and they will ensure that your house is free of clutter. For instance, in the movie '*Blended*', Drew Barrymore is a closet organizer! But why do you think that there is so much clutter in your life? The truth behind this is very surprising! You are unable to say no. You are unable to tell yourself to stop! You find it terribly difficult to say no to something you are very keen on buying.

This clutter has caused psychologists to conduct thorough

research on people. The next chapter deals with the psychology behind clutter. Psychologists believe that there are close to four million Americans who never throw anything away! There are other people who are right behind them in line. They can never seem to stop buying and storing! This reminds me of a scene from '*27 Dresses*'. Katherine Heigl has been to 27 different weddings and has made it a point to store all the dresses and the accessories in a closet. She could have used up all the space in that closet for something worthwhile.

Try this experiment! Sit in the center of your office, room or your house and answer the questions that have been mentioned below. They are simple yes or no questions.

   a. Is the room I am in calm and relaxing? Do I find it beautiful to live or work in? Can I start working on my dreams in this room?
   b. Is it easy for me to invite my friends over to my house without having to think twice?
   c. Do I find what I need with ease? Do I know where I have left my things?
   d. Is there paper lying around the house? Or is it filed away neatly?

Did you find yourself saying no to any of the questions mentioned above? If you have said no, then you will have to set aside a date in your calendar to begin organizing yourself. This book helps you learn how to do this in just seven days!

Why do you want an organized home?

This section covers a tiny exercise that will help you understand why it is essential for you to have a clean and organized home.

When you have come back from work and have had a warm

bath, go to a place that is quiet and relaxing. Sit back, throw your legs onto the table and relax. Try to view your home in your mind. Do you see it disorganized? Now ask yourself why you love having a home that is organized. Begin by listening to what your mind is telling you. Then try to see how these thoughts turn your house into an organized home. When you visualize yourself in a home that is organized, try to see how that has made you feel.

Now try to see how you would like to have your room, house or your office organized. Is there a particular way in that you would want to organize things? Are there things that you have got rid of? Were there any objects that you moved from one place to another? Did you do something to make yourself feel better? When you move objects around in your room, you will find that they make you feel very energetic or gloomy. This is based on Feng Shui. The last chapter in this book deals with a few Feng Shui tips you could use at home to ensure that your house is always bright and lively!

Try to identify your big picture

Human beings in general love telling stories. They love it more when there is a pattern that has been established. Look at all the stuff that you have at home. There is a story that exists behind every object is there not? If there were no story, then you would not have made sure that the object was safe inside your house. Otherwise, it would have been out the window ages ago. You and every other human being have a problem where you cannot let go of objects. You find that you tell every person the same reason why you have an object that you have no need of. When you look at your house from an outsider's perspective, you find it messy and disorganized. This leaves you feeling depressed about your house. You forget that your house is supposed to be your castle and that you have to feel like royalty at home! It is your one sanctuary from the crazy world that exists out there.

You need to realize that change is important. You need to change the stories that you have in life and make new ones. You have to see the big picture in order to ensure that you identify what you really want. Only when you do that will you be able to make any change to your life to get what you desire most.

The biggest problem that human beings have is that they have the brain of an Early Man but they live in the time when there is a constraint on space! This is the blatant truth! Early men used to collect sticks and boulders to ensure their security and sense of survival. In this time, human beings collect shiny new toys and objects that will help them obtain this level of security.

Here is another small activity that you will need to conduct. Try to answer these questions honestly. When you are working on the answers to these questions, try to identify the level and the depth of your emotions and any thought that may pass through your mind.

1. Where is the clutter in your house?
2. When did it get there?
3. How was it brought there?
4. Is there a reason why it is still there?
5. Where does the clutter essentially belong?
6. When an outsider questions you on your clutter at work or at home, how do you respond to them?
7. If you did not have the story about how disorganized you were, who would you be?
8. Would you recognize yourself if you did not have a chance to tell a person how organized you are?

What did you feel when you were answering the questions above? Did you have 'I do not know' as an answer to any of those questions? Did you find yourself feeling ashamed? Did you find yourself feeling anger or guilt? Do you find yourself worrying about the condition of the objects you own? Do you find it scary to think of how you will be able to organize all these objects and ensure that they are kept in the same way? Then you have come to the right place! Welcome to the world of 'When did my house get this disorganized? How do I organize the clutter? Will I be able to ensure that the objects stay organized forever?' You can be rest assured that you are not alone in this! There are 4 million other Americans and maybe another 20 million people from across the world are sailing in the same boat.

Reasons why you need to declutter!

There are numerous reasons why you will have to work on decluttering your house. This section covers the most important reasons. You may have guessed them already. This section confirms all your doubts about why you will need to organize and clear away the clutter.

Reason 1 – Control your need for buying and storing

People are easily frustrated when they find that their belongings are going out of hand. They find it difficult to control and organize the belongings and possessions that they have. They begin to complain and start feeling guilty. They find that they have piled all their belongings up till they find it overwhelming to even think about cleaning it. They find it easier to ignore their belongings. They then start stuffing their belongings into different nooks corners of the house when they finally give up! There are so many people out there who would rather have their house crash down or collapse. They would love for that to happen since they would never have to clean their house again! They find themselves stressing about the clutter instead of dealing with it. Some people would even prefer death to the clutter they have at home.

There are people who have the habit of collecting items that are worthless to them. They have a need to buy things when they enter a store. And when there is a sale, they are in wonderland! This is ruining their lives in a terrible manner. Such people will need the support of the people around them. There are a lot of groups for clutterers. There are many states that have a group called the '*Clutterers Anonymous*'. This is a program that guarantees a recovery in twelve steps.

There are people all over the world who have become frustrated at themselves for accumulating things in their house. They find themselves with heaps of things that they never use. They also have piles of clothes and objects that are overflowing from the cupboards. These people are often overwhelmed by the level of disorganization in their homes. There has never been a case where a person has deliberately burnt down his house in order to get rid of the clutter. There have however, been cases where people have bought the house right next to theirs in order to get away from all the clutter. This is no healthy way to deal with it! This book helps you understand how you can ensure that your house is decluttered and organized in a week's time!

Reason 2 – You should own your possessions

You have to know that life is short and every moment is precious. People struggle when they have a lot of clutter at home. This book tries to help you avoid the struggle through the decluttering process.

Life needs to be fun and full of joy! The things you own have to bring you a lot of joy and fun. There are people all around you who may complain about the clutter in their house. You may also complain about the clutter in your house. When you find yourself complaining, ask yourself these two questions:

1. What if your house actually burnt down today? Would you miss anything if you lost it?
2. Let us assume that your house was burning down right now. You were given 60 seconds to protect your belongings and drag them out of your house. Do not worry; your family and your purse are safe. What would you choose?

Once you are done answering these questions, try to rate those answers on a scale of one to ten. Do you find that there are certain objects that have made the list? If you find yourself faced with such a tragedy, you would not be able to find what you need most during the rush! What if there was an earthquake or floods? Your house would have come crashing down. You cannot think about how you had wanted to organize the house before so that you could find your papers now could you? This is where decluttering comes in!

Reason 3 – You need to live an uncluttered life

You have to remember that you have the right or the permission to obtain what you need or release what you do not need into the universe. This is the only way you will be able to experience the best life possible.

Here is a small story for you! There was a man who had a huge house that was full of his family heirlooms and other antique items. This man was a veterinarian and had always dreamt about becoming a travel vet. But he could not do that since he had a house that was full of his family's heirlooms. He did not know how anybody in his family would react had he sold the house. But one day he had come home from work to find his entire house burnt down. The firemen were staring at the house feeling bad that there was nothing they could salvage. When the reporters asked the man about how he was feeling, he told them the truth. He did find it a shock, but he realized that now he had no obligation towards the house. He was free to do whatever he wanted to!

There are times when people let go of things that are good or bad for them. This is the only way they will be able to bring in the best into their lives. The road to achieving this may be scary and dark. But if you persevere, you will find that you are happy where you are once you have taken the path.

There is another story about a man who used to collect art and different artifacts from Haiti. He was fascinating by the place and always tried to keep a piece of it with him. A few years later his house burnt down and the man now stays in Haiti!

There is a popular metaphor that is used in Buddhism. This is about the finger and the moon. When a man points at the moon for the moon, he can view both his finger and the moon. But the finger is more prominent than the moon. But when the person looks beyond the finger and at the moon, he will find that he cannot view his finger at all.

This goes to show that no matter how much a person has or does not have, no matter how much he can get more of, he has to realize that he needs to find peace, joy and happiness in the stuff that he owns. Also, these belongings have to be of use to him. The story about the man who collected arts and artifacts from Haiti has finally begun to look beyond his finger and at the moon, which is Haiti. If you take that one extra step towards the moon, you will find that you have found the moon and have become the moon. You will find that you do not have the need to obtain things that make you happy. When you find that your possessions have become heavy and have started to overwhelm you, you have to remember to let go. It is only then that you will find yourself happy.

What if you had an organized life?

This is a question that you may have. You may wonder what you would do with all the time you had if your environment were organized.

Here is your answer. Let us assume that you have an organized life. This implies that you have a lot of time on hand. Use this time to have some fun! You could work on hobbies and passions that you never had time for earlier. Spend time with your friends and family. Make new memories and new connections. You would now have more fun stories to tell people instead of having to tell them about your clutter! Three cheers for yourself!

Chapter 2: The Psychology Of Cluttering

Psychologists have stated that cluttering is a habit that most human beings possess. This is because they are in a trance. Psychologists have said that human beings need to snap out of their trance if they want to live fulfilling lives. This chapter talks about the different ways to snap out of the trance.

As mentioned above, human beings are in a trance. They do not seem to find it strange that they are living in a house that is terribly messy. They walk past their mess and clutter like it is a part of their daily life. You would not be surprised if you walked past your clutter one morning and wished it a good morning. It is probably only then that you will realize that you are in a trance and you need to snap out of it soon! This chapter deals with the trance that you are in and how you must snap out of it.

Move out of your trance

You need to try to move out of your trance soon! It is only when you do that will you be able to make new choices for yourself.

Have you ever walked into a store with a list in your hand but have walked back home with a packet full of things that were not on the list? Have you bought food, clothes or even other items and have wondered when you had bought them? Have you walked into a room for a purpose and forgotten why you had walked in? Have you consumed your meal and wondered when you had consumed it? When you had begun to declutter a pile, did you faze out and walk away from the pile? Did you find yourself in another room with no idea when or why you went there? This is something every human being experiences on a regular basis.

A trance is a state of consciousness that has been altered. This is the state of your mind when it is disassociated from the normal forms of consciousness. When there is a person who is in a trance, he may be experiencing intense brain waves. His brain may also have a lot of intellectual activity. But it is during these times that the person is not physically aware of what he is doing. He is not entirely awake during these times.

When it comes to decluttering, you will find that it is difficult for you to let go and make a change. You will find it difficult to get rid of your inner, outer and other clutter since you are unable to make any decisions or take any actions against the same. This is what makes you equally put off dealing with the issues that are right in front of you. You will not be able to deal with the piles of clutter that are right in front of you. You try to stay indecisive and begin procrastinating. You will find yourself under stress and facing certain levels of discomfort and chaos. You may go for decades thinking that you would do it later.

These trances are created by you. You have done the same thing for so many years and have created a certain routine for yourself. This routine contains all your thoughts, behaviors and beliefs. These trances and routines can be created by you when you are under grief or have faced a loss. All you need it a nudge that will shake you pretty bad.

When you are working towards shaking yourself out of a trance, use the following exercise.

Exercise

Imagine yourself in a third world country. You have absolutely nothing with you. You have a hut that has broken down. There are no doors and only partial walls. There is no trace of electricity. You have no clothes but a sari that has been wrapped loosely around you. You have two bowls and spoons. You also have a bucket. You need this bucket to obtain water for yourself. The only source of water for you is a mile away from where -you are. You have no money and seldom get food. You seldom have a job, but that job does not give you the feeling of security. You need to hunt every single day for food. You will need to look for stones and twigs for the fire to cook your food. You have to do this on a regular basis.

Once you have imagined this, try to move into the next scenario. You are in another third world country. You have a lot more clothing in this country. You have a change of clothes for a week. But your house is decaying. You have a considerable increase in the amount of food. There is a water source in the area you are living in. There is however, no electricity and no money. There are some animals in the area you live in. You still have no job.

Are you done with imagining that scenario? Now assume

that you are in an Amish community. You still have no electricity. But, you have a lot of good clothes, shoes, a home and good furniture. You have a good amount of water. Everything that you own has been built by your bare hands. You do not have a lot of money but have a large community. You also have a great group of friends and have jobs and responsibilities. These responsibilities are towards your family and your community.

Now that you have imagined such a scenario, let us move into the modern era. In this time, you have a lot of money and jobs too! You are taken care of in a very simple and enjoyable manner. You have an environment that is secure. You can also consider the other levels of freedom that you experience in such an era. You have the chance to experience wealth, health, and security. You are able to ensure that you are safe in every nook and corner of the environment.

Now that you have visualized these four lives, get back to your life. See how you are living in your home. How is your office? How are the rooms in your house? Visualize them very carefully. Concentrate on every minute detail.

It is terribly easy to forget that there are different ways in which a person lives in the world. If you have travelled around the country or the world, you will find that people everywhere are experiencing lives that are in great contrast to yours. Only when you travel will you be able to gauge what you have when compared to the other people and what you do not have when compared to them. It is easy to stay wrapped up in your cocoon of perceived reality.

When you have undergone the guided imagery that has been provided above, you may sit quiet for a very long time. This is because you have visualized your life in different scenarios.

You may scream out and say that you would like to live in the Amish country. You may however not want to but the idea that you have been able to get out of your regular trance and have had the time to experience what it would be like to live there is an achievement. You will be able to emotionally go to places you have never been to before. You will be able to see that it is lovely to let go of things around you. It is lovely to go to a place you have never been to before. You are finally able to let go of everything around you and have thought about it during the imagination.

You may have a different view on the guided imagery that you have been asked to go through. It may or may not have helped you initially. But over time you will find that this helps you begin clearing out your clutter. You will be able to let go of certain things in your life. You will be able to simplify the environment you are living in. This will help you feel lighter and happier.

When you are going through the book and working on decluttering, repeat the exercise mentioned above. You have to know how it feels to have nothing. Do you like how you feel there? Do you love the open spaces? Do you like having little to take care of? Now look at the piles of accumulated possessions – your possessions. See how they have been brought into your house. Look at how they have begun to invade your space and your time. Now think about this. Is there anything you would be happy to live without?

How do your shake out of your trance?
The progress in technology and the ability of being at any store on the internet has created a craze in the people. Human beings have been given too many choices and a lot of information. They also have too much money and have no focused strategy on how they can use that money. There are

different online sales that have made people shop like there is no tomorrow. The *'Anything you can buy for a dollar'* sales have their own place. But these sales have turned people into hypnotic zombies. They will do whatever it takes to shop! People have walked into stores during sales and have dumped whatever they could find into their shopping carts. Once they are done with the billing, they dump all the items into plastic bags. These bags are then thrown into a corner of the house and never looked at for quite some time. Or people pick out what they love most from the bag and ignore the rest of the items.

You have to learn how to make the shopping an activity that was planned in advance. This is a pain for some people. But there are people who have never heard of this before. They find it difficult to plan and assign a certain budget to their needs. They are unable to limit their need of buying what they require most. It may seem like a withdrawal from a drug for them.

There are different types of addiction; buying and shopping is one of them. People are addicted to shopping in a way that it has become a drug for them. They NEED to shop irrespective of whether or not they have enough money. These people are called *'Shopaholics'*. The truth is that you should not worry about what objects you are purchasing and bringing into the environment. You have to worry about how these objects make you feel and how many of those very objects have you purchased. It could be a sale or a commercial street; there is no difference if you purchase more either here or there! The amount of things you purchase is because of your inner clutter. You provide yourself with the satisfaction and mental strength only when you have purchased a lot of items. Your need to consume is insatiable. You find the need to fill conversations and the space in your house up with materialistic objects. You have forgotten how to enjoy what you have. You have forgotten that you need to lead a simple life. This has become a habit for most people in the world. They have led themselves into a hypnotic trance.

How to Avoid Purchasing unnecessary stuff?

This section provides you with a list of things you can ask yourself. These questions should help you step out of your trance. You have to ask yourself these questions before you buy any objects or items – whether it is online or offline. You have to ask yourself these questions even if you are at a garage sale. When you find yourself reaching out for items in a shop, ask yourself these questions. You can start by removing the items you WANT but not NEED from the list!

1. Will I be able to afford this item? Do I really think I will be able to? (When you go out for shopping, start carrying cash with you. Avoid using your credit, debit or master cards!)
2. Will I really use this item?
3. Will I need it right away or is it for the future?
4. If I do buy the item, where will I leave it?
5. Is there something that may happen to me if I do not buy the item now?
6. Why is it important for me to own this particular item?
7. Why do I believe that I need the item?
8. Will I be alright, will I be able to live without this item?
9. If I do not buy this item now, will I be able to spend the money elsewhere?
10. If I just save the money now, will I be able to use it on something better?

When you have clutter and continuously buy, the question 'Why do people always complain that they do not have enough money but still buy things?' arises. If you walk into any person's house, you will find that they have a lot of items in the house that they do not need. Some items have never been used by them. They do not care about the other items or have no idea how to use them. There are times that they have lost the objects in their house. This shows that the clutter you have is not just outer clutter. The majority of the clutter you have is because of your inner clutter.

Chapter 3: Defining Clutter!

You began the book with trying to understand how to identify if you have clutter at home. But have you ever thought about what clutter is? There are multiple definitions to clutter. You can pick up any dictionary that is lying at home to know what the definition of clutter is. Or you could just walk up to a closet in your house and you would know what the definition is! This section offers you three definitions that will help you gather a clear picture on what clutter is.

Clutter is the heap and pile of unwanted things that have been accumulated and cause immense confusion and disorder.

Clutter can also be defined as the items that you perceive as causing a disturbance or interfering in your life. These items are the ones that have kept you at bay from what you most want. You may find that you have forgotten about things that are of value to you because of the clutter.

Clutter is a luxury! Yes that is what it is. It is the luxury that you purchase and store. But this luxury gets pushed aside and forgotten after a point of time. It can also be termed as obsessive luxury. This is what you are not supposed to keep with you if you value the balance in your life. You may or may not be able to afford this luxury. But you forget, in your excitement, that this luxury affects your entire life.

The above definition is the truth about what clutter is. In simple terms, clutter is a lot of distraction.

Mostly, clutter is a distraction.

The three types of clutter

When you have worked on organizing your life multiple times, you find that you have categorized your clutter into different boxes. But there exist only three forms of clutter! The three types are explained in detail in this section in the chapter. The explanations provide you with the reasons on how they keep you stuck to what you do not need and restrict the flow of the joyous energy. This section also helps you identify how you can change all of that. There are three types of clutter – the inner, outer and other clutter.

Inner Clutter

What do you think the inner clutter is? It is the clutter that lives in between your ears! This clutter has been there within you since you were born, maybe even before that! This clutter is the web of emotions, opinions, thoughts, beliefs and your perceptions towards life as a whole.

The greatest threats are not the terrorists. The threats are not the different diseases that have been spreading. The threat to your life is a person you know best – you. This person has lived inside your head all your life. You are the commander to this inner self. Your inner self is often cluttered, out of control and chaotic. But this inner self is what controls your entire life! You have to step up and take charge before it is too late for you. You will need to be very conscious of the information that is being absorbed by your inner self. You have to also be careful of the output and the continuous flow of thoughts and ideas. You have to ensure that you will need to use all the energy that you use for these thoughts for something worthwhile.

Outer Clutter

This is the clutter that is material. It includes all the stuff in your environment. This is the stuff that you believe is important for your survival though it may not be true. You however, purchase these items and store them till they become clutter.

Other Clutter

This type is the people and your relationships with them. What if you were asked about your family and friends? Let us assume that your family and friends were not your family or your friends for now. You would be hesitant to answer that question. But when you do, you will find that you have a greater chance of saying no if you are being honest.

There are certain people you know who are the best people to be with! They love you for who you are. But there are other people who are downright mean and evil! They are exhausting to be around since they use up all your good energy! You may find that some of these people are dangerous! You will need to learn to build healthy relationships with your family and your friends. You will also need to draw the boundaries for these relationships. This is to ensure that you live in good health. You have to learn to declutter some of your friends and your family. This is a very tough decision for you to make. But this also makes you brave. It is essential that you do this in order to get your life back on track! You will be able to strike a balance in your life too!

The three types of clutter often overlap. You will need to begin decluttering these clutters one after the other. There are times when you may have to work on decluttering more than one clutter. Do not worry about that and keep forging ahead!

How the types of clutter affect you

As mentioned above, clutter is distracting. It is dangerous or even hazardous at times. There are certain things that these types of clutter effect.

- They use up all your good energy
- The clutter uses up all your time. You keep wondering if there is something you can do about the clutter and end up wiling your time away.
- You lose your power to make any decisions
- You will lose your earning power since you start splashing your money on the outer clutter.
- Your clutter has a direct impact on your regular finances.
- You may begin to perceive yourself negatively.
- Your plans will change drastically
- You will begin making terrible choices
- Your clutter will change how the people around you perceive you.

You may lose important checks and papers in the clutter. There are times when you may have defaulted on a bill because you believed that you had put the bill right on top of the table!

The need for focus

This is the main aspect that you will need to consider. Your question now may be what it is that you have to do with this clutter! This book helps you understand all that! You will learn what it is that you need to do in order to ensure that your house is decluttered and organized. There are tips that have been provided to you in this book that will help you bring your life back on track. You will be able to get rid of the inner, outer and other clutter with ease.

You may want to put off the decluttering because you are worried about how frustrated you may get. You may want to put it off for a day. Soon this day will become a week and then maybe a year. Here is a mantra that you can follow to ensure that you become focused! You should not worry about what will happen if you die tomorrow. Instead, worry about how it would be to live the way you are living now for the next twenty or thirty years.

I am sure you can do it! You need to do it because you deserve it! You should never settle for what you think you deserve. You need to always aim for higher.

Why are you going to try organizing your clutter?

You may have already decided that your clutter needs to be organized. Have you thought about why it is necessary that you do? Is it because of the reasons mentioned in the book? There is a deeper need of why you need to organize the clutter in your house. This section covers those reasons.

Yourself

You love your house and you love the immediate environment. You would not have bought the house for yourself if you did not like it. When you had purchased the house you had a vision of how you would want it arranged.

You always dreamt of inviting your friends over to your house. When your house is organized, you will experience very little stress. You will find yourself with more time. This helps you enjoy the little joys in life. You will be able to have a more balanced life.

Family

When your house is disorganized, you will find yourself stressed. This stress is often passed onto your family. This leaves all the members in your house feeling stressed. When your house is organized, you will find your family living a stress free and a happy life.

Children

You may have children at home or may want to have some more. If you are organized at home, you will be able to provide a role model for your children. They will learn how to be organized. They will only learn through chores and other responsibilities.

Successors

It is a fact that you will die at some point in the future. This is how the life works on the planet. When you are organized, you will be able to handle all your finances with ease. You will also be able to predict the future incomes and will be able to make decisions. You will find it easier to save up money for the future.

You would have paid attention to the fact that your friends and other visitors have not made the list. The fact of the matter is that your house is YOUR house. You need to make it comfortable for you to live in. Your friends and other visitors must enter your homes if they want to. They should not visit you based on what your house LOOKS like.

Chapter 4: Why Do We Have Inner Clutter?

Are you a person who sits and makes To Do lists for yourself? Have you noticed that these lists have never been completed? There are three other things that happen when it comes to your To Do lists.

1. You cannot find the list anymore, although you are sure you have left it where you think you had left it
2. The list is so long that you cannot think of how to get it all done. Reading the list makes you feel horrible about yourself
3. You have written the same lists over and over again but have never bothered to finish the list

This book helps you identify your To Do lists and helps you get them done! Does that make you happy? You can go ahead and do your happy dance!

Layers of Problems cause clutter

There have been many studies conducted by the Mayo Clinic. These studies have stated that being disorganized is the third most stressful thing in your life! This stress can kill you! Ninety seven percent of the time when you visit the doctor because of a headache or a stomachache, it is because of stress! There was a recent news report that stated that the fourth largest contribution to disabilities was stress. It was also forecasted that this rank could drop to the second rank!

You can now say that clutter is not found only due to the lack of organizing skills but also due to stress. It is one of the most important symptoms for stress. Clutter forms a loop with stress, depression, grief, fear, trauma and so on. The best way to deal with this is to work on organizing this clutter! It is only then that you will be able to stop any kind of madness from taking over you.

There are many factors that cause stress. But when it comes to clutter, stress is caused only be a few factors. These factors are:

1. Easy distractions. You find it terribly difficult to focus
2. You will find it difficult to give time to deal with all the mess
3. You are unable to understand how to organize the mess
4. When it comes to deciding what to do with the clutter, your mind is a blank page
5. If you do make a decision, you do not act upon it.

When you find that your life lacks focus and clarity, both Inner and Outer, you will be distracted easily and can be led off your path within no time. You have to remember this German proverb to ensure that you are able to work on your clutter.

'*The main thing is to keep the main thing the main thing*'.

Right now the main thing in your life is to stay focused, you have to remember to keep what you desire most and need most in the center of your attention. Make sure that you take some time every day to identify what the important things you need to do are. Once you have done that, you need to start working on it!

This book will help you focus on getting yourself organized. You will find that if you have begun to organize the things at home, you will be able to organize your office and your mind. You will find yourself with minimal amounts of stress and will be at peace with your surroundings. You will begin to view your life very differently. You will find that there is positivity in every aspect of your life.

Now that you have the control on being organized, you will find that you do not have to go to any clinic to get your stress treated. You have to begin challenging yourself! When you go through this book, start pushing yourself. Make sure that you attack the piles and the lumps one at a time. You will be able to get it done with ease!

The next section deals with a simple technique that you can use to overcome inner clutter.

FOCUS

FOCUS is an acronym that stands for *'Feelings Of Clarity Under Stress'*.

In life you will always be under some kind of stress. That is how life works. There are cases where the constant stress always pulls you away from what you consider truly important in your life. When some event occurs in your life, you find your emotions and thoughts going wild. This is why you need to ensure that you keep yourself detached from these emotions. You will need to keep your inner self, that is your mind and thoughts focused. You have to clear away any types of stressful situations that you may have in life. It is only then that you will be able to stay focused on what you goals are. When you are focused you will be able to move from one step to the next with ease.

FOCUS can also stand for *'Follow One Course Until Successful'*. It is always good to ensure that you stay on one course. You will be able to ensure that you complete the course through your plan of action. You will also be able to learn where you are heading. You have to ensure that you do not jump from one step to the next step without finishing the ones in the middle. There are times when you may have jumped from one step to the next without finishing either step! Try to avoid that to the best of your ability.

You have to remember that you can only ensure that you are focused now. You cannot say that you will be focused tomorrow or day after. The moral is that you must never let your clutter and your disorganization blur your focus or stress you out. You may find yourself off track very soon in that case. This will only add to the pile of frustration that you have faced in that day!

There are clear steps that you can follow to ensure that you do not have any chaos or disorder in your life. You will need to ensure that organization is your priority. You will need to commit to this to ensure that your life is on the right track. You have to start right now. Begin giving yourself time to declutter. Start organizing your house for good. It is only when you get back all your space will you find yourself happy and stress free.

Self – inquiry for inner decluttering

As mentioned above, inner cluttering occurs only when a person is unable to get rid of the emotions and thoughts that he has. This section helps you identify the different ways in which you will be able to ensure that you are decluttering your inner clutter. You can ask yourself these questions and when you know the answers, you can then work on how to declutter.

1. What are the changes that you will need to make to yourself? How do you ensure that there are positive changes that you can make to your life?
2. What are the things you will need to let go of? Will letting go of these things help you enjoy your life more?
3. If you organize something in your life, will you be able to give yourself some more free time?
4. What is that one thing that would give you more space in your house if removed?
5. Is there a certain thing in your life that is scaring you or stressing you out? If you removed that from your life would you be able to make positive changes to your life?
6. Is there a story that you keep telling people? About why your house is disorganized? Would you like to stop telling people that story?
7. What is the new story that you would want people to know?
8. Is there a reason why having a house full of stuff has kept you from enjoying your life?
9. How would you feel if your house burnt down? What if you lost whatever you owned due to some natural disaster?

10. What if you lost everything except for your important documents, wallet and family?
11. Would you live any differently?
12. How would you react? What would you say?

Why do we have clutter?

This is a question that every person needs to answer! Why is it that you have clutter at home? There are many reasons why. But the most important reason is that you can own the clutter!

This section covers some of the main reasons why you have clutter at home or at office.

1. You buy more than required
2. You do not know how to store the stuff you have in a functional manner
3. When you have different systems at home, you do not know how to corral the stuff using the systems
4. You do not know how to organize your stuff
5. You claim to never have enough time to organize the stuff
6. You never have enough space to organize the stuff because you have overwhelming amounts of it!
7. You find that you have no energy left to store the different items
8. You initially find too much space and have the need to fill all those spaces up
9. You require a lot of help. But ego comes in the way. You never ask another person to help you.
10. You will blame it on your genes. You will state that you come from a family where organization is not important. You have hence not learnt how to do the same.
11. You state that organizing is not important to you

12. You may have the notion that if you do not declutter, there are no grave consequences that you will have to face
13. You have not made the decision to get organized yet
14. You have not decided to take action
15. You have become a rebel. You have no intention of changing
16. You have got used to it and find it terribly easy to walk over piles without thinking twice

You should know that the outer clutter that you have accumulated is because of your inner clutter. This is because your unconscious mind has programmed you in such a way that you have to constantly buy things for yourself. There are people all across the world with the mentality that they have to shop till they drop. If there are sales around town, they will splurge all their money on a pair of boots or heel that they may be able to wear with only one dress. These people have lost track of the important things in their lives. They have also lost track of the fact that they could do so much more with the time and energy that they spend on this maniacal shopping. The amount of money that can be saved for the future is a large sum too!

These people had come into picture after the Second World War! They were made to create and produce goods. They were also created to consume those goods. These people obliged to the rules and conformed to them. It is those very rules that are killing them now. It has been said that the Americans spend close to four hours of shopping every day. That is more than forty percent of the time the people in other countries spend on shopping. There are a million advertisements a day that tell you and the other viewers that you need to purchase some goods in order to be happy. If you did not obtain these goods you were living life all wrong!

There are billion advertising and marketing agencies that have taken over the advertising of a few products. They claim in their advertisements that if the person buys their product, they will be happier, richer and prettier than what they are now. Human beings buy into all this façade with ease. That is how their unconscious has programmed them.

Your children may watch some advertisement on television or may have come across it in a magazine. This advertisement may be about the different toy sets that are available in the market. They will throw tantrums till they get the toy. But how many toys do your children need? Do they need so many clothes and shoes? Do they need the clothes that they have never used before? Why are there so many clothes in their closets that have never been worn? Why are there clothes with the tags on? Why are there heaps of clothes in the back of their cupboard? You will be surprised that even the poorest of people have clothes that have been stocked. This is because they can!

Think about this. What if you were a resident of a Third World Country? What if you did not have the money, the closets, the walls or even a roof to live under? Even in such a situation, it is not difficult to have clutter. This is indeed a very strange problem. What if you were living in Bangladesh or Nepal? Would you be worried about the clutter or the mess in your life? Or would your life be very different from what it is now?

Chapter 5: Project Declutter!

This chapter deals with the different ways you can try to motivate yourself to work towards decluttering your house. However, you have to first identify why you have clutter in your house.

What are the reasons for cluttering?

There are a million reasons why you or any other human being clutters. You can always come up with a reason if asked. This section covers the most common reasons why human beings declutter. You can try to identify why you clutter through the reasons mentioned here. You can also come up with a few other reasons, reasons why you clutter.

1. You may have the feeling that you will need it immediately after you throw it out
2. You will find that the items that you want have are good enough to use even though they are not in a very good condition
3. The item was a gift, so you will not want to throw it out

4. When the person who gives you the gift visits you, you do not want them to feel bad about not having the item with you any longer
5. You will feel bad about throwing an item out if you know that it is expensive
6. The item is brand new. It has never been used.
7. If there is an item that is broken, you have the feeling that you will fix it soon!
8. When it comes to clothes, you will tell yourself that you will fit into the clothes when you lose weight. You have to remember that the clothes should fit you and it is not the other way around.
9. The clothes that you may throw out now may come back into fashion.
10. You may have loved what you have and are unable to get rid of it.
11. You got it for free and are unable to part with it!

There are many other reasons why you are unable to get rid of your clutter. Identify those reasons and start getting rid of the items.

But there are other reasons that people usually give when they are asked why they love leaving their house disorganized. You may have given people some of these answers too!

1. I do not have enough time to work on all the clutter. I have deadlines at work and need to take care of the other things at home too!
2. There is absolutely no space in my house for the items. They hence need to be piled one on top of the other
3. I need someone to help me with moving the items in order to sort them out

4. I have no idea how this has to be done. I do not know where to start
5. I have no knowledge on the different systems that can be used to declutter.
6. I do not have the finances to buy the system or hire someone to help me organize my house

There are other reasons why a person would not want to organize their clutter. This is because of their minds.

1. They claim that they do not have the energy to work on the clutter at home
2. They do not have the will power to do it
3. They may have no motivation to work continuously on organizing their house

Every person can relate to these reasons at one point or the other!

The two important steps to organize clutter

You have come across the different reasons why you or any other human being has decided to avoid decluttering. But when you know the reasons why, you will have to learn on how to get your clutter under control. The two main reasons why you are unable to do that are:

1. You are unable to make a decision
2. You have avoided taking action and have not moved the clutter ever

Here is when you will have to make your very own to do list! You will have to work on ensuring that you complete the list and that your clutter has been sorted. There are two steps that you will have to fulfill in order to get this done.

Decide

You may have a lot of clutter at home. The first thing you must do is decide to change the clutter. You will need to decide to move the clutter and organize it! How will this happen? This will only happen when you DECIDE on a time to organize the clutter and DECIDE on how you are going to do it. You have to DECIDE how you are going to keep your clutter and also where it is going to go. When you have made all these decisions, you can move into the next step.

Action

Most people always make decisions all day long. They decide that they have to clean and organize but never get around to it. There are other decisions that are small, like putting your linens in a closet or cleaning your couch. You can decide to do them, but it getting around to doing it that is the most important! When you make a decision, you have to learn how to stick to it! If you hesitate or are afraid, or begin to procrastinate you will derail all your decisions. It is between the decision that you take and the action that you make where the trance lies. The gap between knowing what to do and performing that action could be because of different reasons. There may be layers of problem that may cause you to avoid taking action. This leads to self – loathing.

So no matter what the decision is, even if it is the smallest action make your decision quickly and work on it!

How to keep yourself motivated while decluttering?

After you have read this book, you would have made notes for yourself. You have now become excited on how you are going to be working on decluttering your house. You now wonder how it is that you are going to keep yourself motivated to do it.

You have no formulae that you can use to keep yourself motivated. Do you like exercising? Do you keep pushing yourself to exercise? That is exactly what you have to do when you are working on decluttering and organizing your house! You just have to do it! You do not have a choice but to do it!

There are some things that you can do!

Give yourself deadlines

You will have to give yourself and your family deadlines. It is always good to do this. At work, you finish work efficiently and on time when you have been given deadlines. The same concept works here. You can push yourself to finish what you have been assigned to do when you have been given a deadline.

Create a declutter Buddy system

Make sure that you create a system where you will be able to ensure that you are checking up on each other when cleaning. Make sure that you have a system where you are checking up on each other when you have to begin decluttering. Work on motivating each other as well!

Chapter 6: Materials To Make You Faster And More Effective

Before you get on your mission of 'clean the house', you must accumulate some of the ingredients that are mandatory for a perfect cleaning process. Ranging from vacuum cleaner to baking soda, get the list of things that you require to keep your house neat and tidy -

Vacuum cleaner
This is the most necessary object to keep your house clean. It helps you in carrying out the most preliminary step of home cleaning - removal of dust. Vacuum cleaner helps you in taking away all the visible debris as well as fine particles of dirt and dust. Regular vacuuming keeps the atmosphere sanitized that also plays positive role in improving the atmosphere and increasing life of rugs, carpets, sofas and other furnishing items.

Mop
This is another basic object that is a must for 'clean your house' project. It is vital to eliminate all the stains and mop

out all the bacteria. There are several types of mops. Some mops are designed to clean the floor while many others are preferred for window and wall cleaning. To make the best use of it, you can dip your mop into a solution of warm water and cleaning liquid.

Windex

Windex is a useful product that is known for its affectivity in cleaning glass items. Therefore, it is included as one of the most important house cleaning products. Windex would help you in removing stains and smudges from glass surface without much effort. All you need to do is to spray it on the surface of windows, doors and other glass made objects and wipe them with a clean cloth.

All-purpose cleaner

An all-purpose cleaning solution is another component that must be there in your cleaning box. It helps in the complete cleaning of house, eliminating all the bacteria along with harmful germs and their power center - dirty stains.

Baking Soda

This is one of the key elements of your kitchen. Now, it is a key object of your cleaning regime too. Baking soda incorporates amazing qualities of removing unpleasant odors. Spill it on your carpets and rugs to make them odor-free.

Microfiber wipes

Yes, they too are important! Microfiber wipe is vital to keep everything around clean and completely dirt-free. Most importantly, these cloth pieces can be washed and re-used.

Gloves

In the process of cleaning, you touch a lot of chemical cleaners as well as use your hands to clean stains and dirt. In this process you come in contact with bacteria and germs. Touching them without using gloves can be risky for your health. Therefore, gloves are supposed as a mandatory inclusion in your cleaning kit. Using a rubber gloves that extends up to your elbow would be the best choice.

Polish

This is the most important and final addition in your neatness drive. Polish is important to finally remove bacteria and germs from house and keep your house as well as its interior new for years.

Apart from these special ingredients, also add some more useful cleaning objects such as lemon, vinegar etc. into your cleaning kit. These organic objects would help you in toxic free cleaning.

Chapter 7: The Feng Shui And Decluttering

When you are working on decluttering your house, you will find that you now have a few items that you have got rid of and may find a good amount of space in your house. When you find the space, it does not mean that you go ahead and fill it up again. You can try to Feng Shui your house up.

What is Feng Shui?
Feng Shui is the practice of arranging the different objects in your house to mirror the emotional turmoil that is happening in your head. Feng Shui is the new way of living. The idea has been grasped from the Chinese philosophy. In short, Feng Shui is the idea of living in harmony with your surrounding environment. The surroundings that are found around you, or the existing surroundings, were divided into the five natural elements in the world. This, after the division, became one of the main principles of the Feng Shui. There are other theories of great importance in the Feng Shui. These practices and principles had been created in 4000 BC. This art of living is followed by many people all

across the world. Most doctors recommend Feng Shui as therapy for their patients. This is because the person finds his mind at ease.

Feng Shui is a type of design therapy. You can design your room or your apartment in a way that it complements its immediate surroundings. This tradition has passed on from generations and went through multiple changes over time. It was only during the third century that the Chinese introduced the idea of Feng Shui all across the world. The Chinese during the West Han dynasty believed that the planet Earth is alive and has immense amounts of energy in it. The energy that the earth contained is called the Chi and is often termed as the Universal Energy. This Chi is often influenced by the geography of the Earth. Therefore, when you are rearranging your house, you will need to ensure that there is a positive energy that is flowing through the house. If you have positive energy in your house, you will be able to keep yourself happy just by entering your house or any room in your house. If you have negative energy, you may find yourself depressed on more than one occasion.

The rich and the poor practice Feng Shui. They have houses that are surrounded by walls and with rich flora and fauna. The houses in China are constructed based on the positive effects of the relationships that existed between the members in the family. There is another theory in Feng Shui called the Yin and Yang theory. The left side of the house is where the male energy force, the Yang, lies while the right side of the house is where the female energy force, the Yin, lies. These energy forces are linked to the Earth's energy. Through Feng Shui, you will be able to strike a balance between the Yin and Yang energies in your apartment or your office.

How do you use Feng Shui for your house?

You can easily Feng Shui up your house once you have decluttered it. You will need to begin considering what you bring into your house. You will have to see how you have arranged the rooms in your house and also the objects within that room. The décor in your house plays a major role in the flow of the energy in the house. You have to remember that every object in your house has a certain amount of energy in it. These could be inanimate objects too! Feng Shui helps in guiding all the energy in the house to flow freely.

Feng Shui tips

This section covers a few ideas that you could use once you have decluttered your home! Let us work on the Feng Shui for your house!

Seating, Shapes and the Spatial Relations

The way you place the different beds in your house and the sofa sets in your living room play a major role in the flow of the energy in your house. This section tries to help you identify the ways in which you would have to set your décor.

The Sofa

The sofa has to always be placed against a wall. You have to ensure that the sofa is not anywhere close to your entrance. It is best if you have a view of the entrance when you sit on the sofa. Leave a little space between the wall and the sofa.

Assume that there is no wall in your living room that can have a place for the sofa. In such a case, try to have a lamp or the Console right behind the sofa. This will help you feel more secure.

The Seating

Let us now talk about the seating in your living room or even on your porch. You have to ensure that there is a good amount of gap between the people when they sit together. You cannot have the chairs so far apart that people cannot talk to each other. If you have the chairs or the couch pushed far back to the wall, people may not want to converse with any person across the room. It is better to have the seats in an intimate arrangement. This will invite people to converse with one another.

Whenever you or any other human being enters a restaurant, he looks for a comfortable place to sit. He would want to have his back facing the wall. This is because they feel safe that they are not exposing their backs to another person. It is always good to let the guests find seats in your house that allow them to face their backs to the wall.

The Tables

The tables are a very important part of the furniture in your living room and in your dining room. You may also want to have tables in your bedroom. A rectangular table or a square shaped table is not conducive to the room. People cannot walk across the room without being conscious of the table. If there are sharp edges to the table, you may hurt yourself while walking past it. It is best to have a table that is circular in shape. The same goes for the tables in your bedroom. If you have tables with pointy edges, you may walk into it and stub your toe pretty badly.

Windows, the Colors and the organized Clutter

This is one section that you would be keen on viewing.

The Windows

The windows in your house play a major role in the flow of the energy. Assume that you have a huge window in your living room right next to the entrance. You do not want the energy from your house to leave through the window. Place curtains on the window to ensure that you can draw the curtains when you find that there is too much heat. There are people who feel that these windows are an invasion to their privacy. In such a case, you will need to ensure that you have the windows shut with dark colored drapes.

The windows in your bedroom also can be viewed the same way. If you have windows that are east facing in your bedroom, try to place your bed opposite that window since it is always good to wake up with the bright sunlight.

There are times when the only view from your window is a brick wall or a pipeline. At such a time, you can use certain items to decorate your window. You could have a crystal hanging on the window. This crystal can redirect all the energy that goes away from the house towards the brick line

The Clutter

Color is a very important aspect of Feng Shui. Once you have decluttered your house, you can find items that you never knew existed! This reminds me of the scene from the book 'Shopaholic takes Manhattan'. In this book, the protagonist, Rebecca Bloomwood goes crazy with shopping in New York. When she gets home, her friend Suze tells her that she should declutter. She must get rid of every item she never uses. She takes up the challenge but finds it very difficult to get rid of her stuff. Instead, she takes the airtight bags and stuffs all her clothes and accessories into those bags. When Suze enters the room, she is surprised to find a marble top table in Rebecca's room! The same could happen with you.

When you have finished decluttering, you can find objects that you had forgotten about and use them to help improve the look of your house. You may have found pictures from school, or from a road trip you had taken in college! You can use all the clutter to decorate your house! You must do this only if you are certain that the clutter does not have to be thrown away!

You may wonder what the point of the exercise of decluttering is then. But here is what you need to remember. You have to make sure that you do not store things that have no meaning to you. When you do this, you will only be left with things you love most. Try to incorporate those into your bookshelf or on your wall! That way you will be able to ensure that you have memories and your house is organized. When you find that there are new things that need to be added, you can always try making a new story line. But assess whether what you are adding is indeed very important for you!

The color

Color is an important aspect to your house. When you have bright colors, you will be able to spread a lot of energy. You can wake up in the morning feeling energized if you have a room that is painted bright yellow or red. Try to avoid any dull colors since they only tend to depress you!

Décor

The décor is another important aspect of your house. You will need to ensure that you get the perfect furniture to match your house. Your dining room area and your kitchen are the most important places since this is where you will obtain your nutrition from.

Let us talk about your dining room. You need to make sure

that the décor in the dining room is more formal. You have to also make sure that the décor reflects who you are as a person and your family as a whole. You can have décor that goes with the wood in your dining area. Try to ensure that you have a round table. However, a rectangular or a square shaped table would not harm anybody since nobody would want to sit at the corner of the table. However, if you find that a round table fits better than a rectangular or square shaped table, you can go ahead and use that! You may want to have a table that is made of wood. Wood helps in connecting you to the earth and will keep you grounded. You can have a carpet in the room since it helps in providing a very intimate atmosphere.

When it comes to the kitchen, you will need to have décor that connects you to the earth. Try to have stone countertops. If you already have the same, work on keeping it clean! You will have to ensure that your cupboards are clean as well!

The next few chapters deal with how you can ensure that you declutter different parts of your house! The order provided here is not the law! It is a blueprint that you can change according to your convenience and needs! There are a few Feng Shui tips at the end of the chapters that will help you organize your rooms in the best way possible. This will ensure that there is good energy flowing throughout your house!

Chapter 8: Monday - Getting Rid Of The Dusts

Dusting is the most basic step of cleaning; therefore, the first day of your keep-the-house clean mission would be devoted to it. Put your mask on, get your vacuum cleaner handy, grab the wipe and pull your sleeves to make your lovely home completely dust free. Looking for tips, browse through the section -

To eliminate all the dust particles from your house, you'll have to follow a strategy. You cannot clean the entire area at once, hence, dedicate separate timing for dusting of each, electronics, cabinets, furniture, soft toys, vents, windows, ceiling fans and areas hidden behind furniture and home-appliances.

Electronics

Electronics such as televisions, computers, stereos, printers are some of the areas in our house that shows the maximum presence of dust particles. If you do not wipe them regularly, they would look like nothing less than dust-bathed electronics. But, these dust particles are very harmful for their longevity, as these tiny particles turn to clog our electronics. To clean your gadgets you can use a micro-fiber wipe and vacuum cleaner. With help of Windex micro-fiber wipes will remove dirt from glass surface of electronics while vacuum cleaner would help in pulling out dust from cords and vents.

Furniture and curio cabinets

We all love furniture and curio cabinets with intricate carvings. But these intricate carvings are the place where dust finds its safest home. You can clean the nook and carving area of furniture and cabinets with help of fine paint brush or makeup brush. After cleaning those hard to clean areas, dust-free these cabinets and furniture with a good wiping cloth.

Carpet, rugs, Soft toys

Baking soda is the best agent to make fabric made objects along with soft toys. You can keep smaller fabric items in a plastic bag and sprinkle baking soda over them. Now close the plastic bag and shake it for a few minutes. Baking soda will remove most of the dust particles. Rest of them can be removed with help of vacuum cleaner. To dust-free bigger fabric made furnishings such as carpets, you can sprinkle baking soda on it and to take clumps of soda out, you can use vacuum cleaner.

In hidden areas

We keep cleaning the areas that are open and visible but dust often gets stored in areas that are normally hidden behind home appliances and furniture. The best way to clean such areas is to remove stuffs which are covering them but in case, you are finding it hard to remove your furniture and larger electronics, you can use a long handled mop dipped in solution water and cleansing powder to make all the hidden places of your house dust and debris-free.

Vents

Windows, vents and doorframes also attract dust. You can clean them with help of microfiber cloth or using an electrostatic mop. To clean window glasses, use Windex spray.

Ceiling fans

Get your step stool, damp a microfiber wiping cloth and clean your ceiling fan. To give the final touch, use a damp paper towel.

Chapter 9: Tuesday - Cleaning The Bathroom

Post the program of dusting, the next step is bathroom cleaning. So, keep your Tuesday free for this... However, it is a big fact that cleaning the restroom area is one of the most annoying tasks but ignoring this part of cleaning is not considered wise. Since washroom is the place where germs tend to make their easy residence, it is crucial to maintain a higher level of hygiene in this area.

For an easy functioning, you can divide bathroom cleaning into following sections.

Clean washroom curtains and mats first

Before you get on the job of proper bathroom cleaning, it is important to remove curtain and mats from this area and wash them clean. You can use solution of anti-bacterial liquid and detergent to clean these objects.

Dirt free your shower

Most of us tend to ignore shower while cleaning the washroom but did you know, it is equally important to keep you healthy? Most of the times, dirt particles and soap froths get clogged in tiny shower holes - making them center of bacterial germination. You can clean shower using a paste of baking soda and vinegar.

Cleaning of tiles, walls and ceiling

The deep-cleaning regime of bathroom includes a complete cleaning session. Hence, you cannot let the wiping of washroom tiles, walls and ceiling go on a toss. To clean all these, you can make use of all-purpose cleaning solution, wiping cloth and micro-fiber mop. First spray the cleaning solution on the entire area. After a few minutes wipe them out. To reach on higher points and ceiling, you can use micro-fiber mop. They work as effectively as wiping cloth.

Cleaning sink and bath-tub

For a healthy living, it is very important to keep sink and bathtub completely free from hazardous microorganisms. Hence, it is always advised to use germ removing liquids to clean them. In absence of anti-bacterial solutions, you can use white vinegar while a paste of baking soda would aid you keeping these two washroom objects stain free. To disinfect faucets, you can use disposable cleaning wipes.

Toilet cleaning

To clean the toilet, you must keep toilet brush and dedicated toilet cleaning solution handy. The easiest way to clean toilet is to spray the toilet cleaner all around the pot and rub it thoroughly with help of toilet brush to eliminate all the germs. This process should be followed with flush and water wash. Dedicated toilet cleaners not only kill germs but also, they remove rigid stains. But if, still there are some stains left on the toilet sheet, you can use bleaching powder to make it shine.

Chapter 10: Wednesday - Cleaning The Kitchen

The place where you cook your food and store all your edibles must be thoroughly neat and 100% germ free. Hence, this cleaning guide has dedicated third day of your 'keep your house clean' schedule to kitchen cleaning. On this Wednesday, take out all the essential cleaning agents to make your kitchen completely dirt-free. Let's do it in following steps -

Get your cleaning sponges ready

The first lesson of kitchen cleaning is to dedicate sponges for each cleaning section. For example, you must use separate sponges for washing dishes, counter wiping etc.

Follow instruction manual to clean appliances

Your kitchen houses some of the most important appliances of your house such as microwave, refrigerators, chimneys, and dish-washer. To clean these electronic goods, you must follow the instruction manual.

Cleaning cook-top

To disinfect the cook-top, you can use a cleaning wipe dipped in the solution of detergent, lemon juice and water. This will aid you in removing hard stains from the cooktop as well as killing harmful germs. To remove caked-on food residues you can use softly use a razor blade or cautiously use hard dish- washing scrubber. While cleaning your cook- top, pay attention to remove all the food residues, as these residues become the soft pad for germs offering them a safe haven for cultivation.

Cleaning the counter top

You do most of your cutting and chopping on the kitchen counter. This is the place where you keep your food too. Therefore, it is very important to disinfect this area of kitchen too. You can use a wiping sponge and clean kitchen counter by damping this sponge into a mix of vinegar and soap water. Vinegar is an organic disinfectant that does not harm your health as chemical disinfectants do.

Cleaning the floor

Are you aware that in numerous Asian countries, people do not take their slippers inside the kitchen area. They do it to keep the kitchen floor away from all the infections that could pave its way in your kitchen from the outer world. Although, keeping your shoe out of kitchen is little hard to practice, you can still keep your cooking area sanitized by regularly cleaning and wiping its floor with help of quality disinfectants

Chapter 11: Thursday - Cleaning The Bedrooms

The bedroom of your house is that special area where you spend some of the most relaxing moments of the day. You come here to put all your tensions off and rejuvenate your mind and soul for the next day. Hence, your bedroom should be highly cleaned. A cleaner bedroom nit only elevates your mood but also it refills newer energy in you. But, how can you easily clean your bedroom. Here are a few tips...

Take out all the furnishings and clean them out

Remove every bit of furnishings from your bedroom, including curtains, bed sheet, pillow covers and mattresses. Wash all the bedroom fabrics with detergent and anti-bacterial liquid to cut down every possibility of harmful germination. To cleanse mattresses, you can use electrostatic cleaner and then keep them for a while under sun. Sunlight is an amazing natural disinfectant which would make your mattresses completely germ free.

Cleaning cabinets and reorganizing them

Your bedroom is the place where you keep some of your most loved souvenirs as well as clothes. The first step of messy to clean room is organizing your respective cabinets. You must keep properly dust your cabinets and keep all your things in place. Once, goodies are back to their original place, you would find a radical change in the over-all appearance of your bedroom.

Clean and polish bedroom furniture

You had been longing to use the polish can kept in your cleaning kit. Now, the time has come to use them. To give a new look to your bedroom, you can apply coats of polish on your bedroom furniture. Polishing endows furniture items with new shine as well as longer life. Your bedroom will be ready for new decor and beautification, once the polish is dried up.

Add the tinge of your favorite aroma in your bedroom

To make your recently cleaned bedroom a cozier area, you can consider spicing it up with your favorite aroma. You can either go for a bunch of fresh flower or consider putting an aromatherapy vaporizer in your bedroom. This will uplift your mood as well as kill the smell that comes from furniture post polishing.

Tips to make bedroom cleaning fun

The moment you enter in your messed-up bedroom, you find it a gregarious task. But how to make your relaxing area look perfect when there is no help around. Grab your phone, make call to the person with whom your feel the most-connected, put the phone on speaker... keep talking and keep working. This way, you would not only easily jazz-up your bedroom, but also you would find it fun to do in company of your loved ones...

Feng Shui tips for your bedroom

Once you have decluttered your bedroom, you can work on organizing and arranging it. You should be able to ensure that there is a good flow of energy in the house!

- Your bed can be moved to ensure that you can approach the bed from both ends
- Place a bedside table on either side of the bed. This leaves you with a sense of security
- Have a night lamp on either table. This will help you illuminate your room when there is too much darkness
- Make sure that the linen you use for your bed and the curtains are bright and vibrant

Ensure that your bed faces a window if possible!

Chapter 12: Friday - Cleaning The Living Room

Fifth day of the week goes to the cleaning of the area where you build most of your memories. Yes, it is living area. This is considerably the broadest and most open area of your house and it accommodates maximum number of furniture and souvenirs. Therefore, living area needs a lot of attention and care while you are on the cleanliness drive. How can you do it an organized manner? Read on to get the details -

Dusting and cleaning of furnishing and upholsteries

The first step of a neat and clean living room is to dust everything around. Since, you are already done with dusting on the first day of your cleaning regime, you can consider a touch-up to avoid any sort of caking up of dust particle. Next, in the line is cleaning and sanitization of all the upholstery objects of living room.

Note - while dusting larger electronics and furnishings of living room, do not forget about sanitization of smaller objects yet important objects of living room such as remote controls, telephone, ashtray, coasters etc. These objects are used more than bigger goods, hence their sanitization is equally important.

Window cleaning

Window is mostly done on the day of dusting but to peep outside from a bright and neat window, you must keep cleaning it regularly. Once again dust the window frames and apply Windex on window glasses (if needed).

Cleaning of fixtures

To make living room more vibrant than other areas of house, use extra lighting. Lighting arrangements brings along use of multiple fixtures too. Hence, now comes the cleaning of fixtures of your living room. If those are beyond your reach, you can use an extendable duster to make them clean.

Vacuum clean drapes, blinds and sofas

Dust tends to hide in the sections of drapes, blinds and sofas. You can use a vacuum cleaner to get these hidden dust particles out and fully sanitize your drawing area.

Dust and clean your souvenirs

To make your living room beautiful, you have put a lot of souvenirs on this area. They are too delicate to clean in a huff. You can consider cleaning them by devoting maximum timing and attentively dusting them. It'll help you in keeping them clean without suffering any damage.

Cleaning of your indoor plants

Indoor plants can found in most of the houses. They add into the beauty of the living area of your house. While you are cleaning your living room, you can dust/wash your indoor plants too and keep them somewhere else under shade for a while. Bring them back once you are over with living room sanitization.

Things to take care of while sanitizing your living room

When you are cleaning, probability is high; you may forget a few essential things to do. Make a note of the points, which must not be ignored while disinfecting and cleansing living room -

- cleaning of internal drawers of furnishing items is equally important as cleaning of their exterior parts.

- spread cleaned carpets and rugs in this area only after floor cleaning.

Feng Shui tips for your living room

Your living room is where you sit with all your guests or with your family for some fun times. You want the living room to be inviting and warm. There are certain things you can do to ensure that the living room is inviting.

- Make sure that your furniture does not point towards the television. Leave it attached to the wall but do not let that be the center of attention
- Have a carpet on the floor since that leaves everybody with a sense of grounding. They will be more open to talking to each other
- Have a table in the center of the room. This table can be used when you are conversing with people
- Make sure that your couch is vacuumed regularly.

Chapter 13: Saturday - Cleaning The Floors

The second last day of your cleaning schedule is kept for floor cleaning. In the present scenario of flashy and attractive floors, there are plenty of floor types. And, you will have to use particular type of cleaning method for each type of floor cleaning. Know, how can you clean each type of floors -

Cleaning of wood floors

Considerably, these are the most glamorous flooring type. They add a special aura of style to your home. And, most importantly, it is very easy to maintain the sheen of these floorings, keeping them completely clean. If you take care of wooden floors regularly, you would not have to worry about life of your floors. But it crucial to keep in notice that life of wooden floors also lies on the type of sealant you use to clean and maintain its shine. Mostly people use varnish, lacquer and shellac. You can give a try to polyurethane too. This offers optimum shine to the wood-made floors and also, you would not require anything extra post the application of polyurethane while after using lacquer and varnish, you may need to use solvent based cleaners to get rid of dirt particles and loose debris. The best way to clean wooden floor is to apply polyurethane or other cleaners after the vacuum cleaning. Post cleaning, use a damp mop to remove extra solvents.

Tiled/Marble floors cleaning

Marble floors are quite fashionable. Apart from floors, marble is also used in bathroom walls and counter tops. Normally, two types of marble floorings are available - polished and unpolished. Unpolished marble floorings are porous in nature and they stain very easily too. Hence, it is advised to not use any sort of varnish or lacquer to clean such floorings, instead, you should consider using specified sealer. Cleaning polished marble floors is little easier. Although, they too can get stained easily but they can be cleaned without hassle if you clean them with a mop damped in the solution of all purpose cleaning liquid and water.

Cleaning of ceramic floors

Ceramic floor is the easiest to clean and maintain. Since, these are artificial substitute of marble flooring, they are devoid of the faults of natural marble flooring. These floorings come with extra glaze; therefore, it is wiser to clean them with mild cleaning solvents than using an abrasive cleanser. Such cleansers may rip off its glaze. Use a flat mop to clean ceramic floors and a ceramic sealer to seal the grout lines.

Cleaning of vinyl floor

Vinyl flooring is also easy to clean and take care of. It can be cleaned with a neutral cleanser. You can use a mop and a mix of vinegar and water bring shine to the flooring. Pouring or scouring water on vinyl flooring is not considered better for its longer life. This may loosen the adhesive of the flooring, detaching it from the surface.

Cleaning of brick floors

Brick floor is also common among people who want to give an exceptional look to their house. But brick floors are porous in nature; therefore you may need to invest a lot of time as well as effort to clean such flooring. Experts advise to use water-based sealers to clean indoor brick floorings. You can use sponge mop to clean brick floors.

Note - while cleaning brick floors, take care that you are not using any hard soaps and tough cleansers. It may damage the surface of brick flooring.

Chapter 14: Sunday - Family Bonding While Organizing

The last day of your cleaning activity has arrived. Now, you can have a cleaner abode where you can relax here lazily. Home cleaning on your own is a hectic affair but with support of family, you can turn it into a lovely family bonding moment. Know about the tips that can help you in turning the tough job of home cleaning a fun activity laden get-together for family people.

Divide jobs of cleaning

It is clear that not everyone enjoys cleaning house but hardly anyone minds cleaning his/her most favorite area in the house. Hence, you must divide cleaning job into sections. It'll help family members to choose his/her preferred areas and clean them easily.

Do not force it on people

A week long cleaning schedule is normally started in the days of holidays. If you forcibly bind your family members in these days of relaxation to clean the house, chances are high the level of frustration may soar up. Hence, instead of forcing it on your loved ones, give them an option. If they happily opt to clean their cabinets and book racks, praise them for it. It'll encourage them in being your cleaning buddy without any qualms.

Make it a fun task

Dust, wipes, mops, vacuum cleaner and so on - cleaning can be an utterly boring activity with these things around. How can you turn it into a fun event? Dividing your family into small groups can be an intelligent idea to make it fun. For example, children can be grouped together to clean book-self and other similar stuffs while you can get help of your mom while cleaning. This will help family members in connecting to each other. You can also sit for family teatime or lunch time to make it more interesting.

Catch up with an old friend on phone while cleaning alone

In your mundane activities, you hardly get any time to connect to your relatives and friends who stay away from you. Make use of your new generation smart phone and catch with one of your old pals while cleaning your house via video calls or speaker phone. This will not only refuel a new energy in you but also you would not be able to realize when you finished the cleaning job.

Treat your family members on the last day of cleaning

The last day of this cleaning schedule falls on Sunday. This day you can lazily relax in your organized and sanitize abode with your family members. Cleaning house had not been this easy without support of your loved ones. Hence, the time has come when you must celebrate the triumphant over messy house... How about ordering pizza for lunch or going out together to spend a lovely evening?

Cleaning can be a great activity to bond with family people while jovially organizing house...

Chapter 15: The Rules To Remember When You Are Decluttering

This chapter will help you remember the few rules that will help you declutter and organize your house effectively.

1. Always decide that you are going to work on decluttering and organizing. You have a lot of clutter around you because you did not make the decision to clean!
2. When you have made a decision, take action immediately. When you have created a schedule for your family to follow while cleaning, ensure that you stick by it.
3. When you have cleared one pile, make sure that you do not go back to that pile again. You have no need to organize if you keep re – piling.
4. When you have decluttered, you would have found items that can be used. Make sure that you use all of that up before you go buy some more. Use ALL of it up!

5. Start using all the stuff you have. You may have stored the crockery in a lot of shelves because you are scared they might break! Use all that up. There is no point owning something if you do not use it.
6. If you think you can reuse the items as something else, go right ahead and do it. If you have a bowl that does not look good anymore but can be used to hold the dishwashing soap in the kitchen go ahead and do that. It is best to use things you have before you buy new items.
7. If you have a lot of things that you are sure you will never use, donate them! There are people everywhere who need those items but have no finances to buy them. See if you can help them! You can also have a garage sale if required.
8. Make sure that every item in your house has a place for itself. The keys have to be in the key bowl and so on. You have to keep track of all the 'homes' of your items. Make sure that your family abides by the rule too! If they have a tough time remembering, you can use sticky notes to label all the homes. This makes it easy to ensure that your house remains clean and organized.
9. If you have a lot of items that you may need immediately, store them in a place where you can find them! What if you had to go to the hospital and have no idea where the keys to your car are? It is best to leave them by the door!
10. Get serious about all your important papers. File them immediately. You do not want to keep them in a safe place and forget all about them till you need them!
11. If you find it very difficult to organize your house, call for help. You need not be afraid that people will judge. You should be proud that you are stepping up and

admitting that you have a problem and that you want to deal with it!

Now that you have memorized those rules, you can begin decluttering! All the best!

Conclusion

House cleaning can be a tedious job if not done in a planned manner. This week long plan will not only help you in cleaning your house in an organized manner but also in a fun-filled manner. Here is a synopsis of the plan on how to go from Monday to Sunday.

Monday - Dedicate this day for dusting. You'll require microfiber wipe, Windex, vacuum cleaner and mops to dust your house. Dusting will include cleaning electronics to keeping loose debris and dirt out from the hidden areas.

Tuesday – The bathroom is one of the most important areas of your house. It should be immensely cleaned. Hence, a full day of Tuesday is dedicated for washroom cleaning. Washroom or restrooms are generally divided in to two segments - bathing section and toilet. It is very important to keep both these parts of bathrooms completely cleaned. While cleaning bathroom, you should also consider cleaning wash basin, faucets and showers to remove any possibility of germ development.

Wednesday - Clean your kitchen on Wednesday. Use instruction manual to clean your home appliances and use natural cleanser such as lemon and vinegar to disinfect cook-top and counter-top.

Thursday - Thursday is for bedroom cleaning. Organize your bedroom furnishing, cabinets and leave a puff of aroma here... You would find your bedroom more comfortable than ever.

Friday - Cleaning living room area can be done on the fifth day of the schedule. You can ask kids of your house to help in this task. They can help you to clean cabinets, souvenirs and furniture while you can concentrate on sanitizing upholstery, windows, fixtures etc.

Saturday - This day is dedicated to floor cleaning. You can consider using different types of cleaning method to clean different types of floors.

Sunday - Cleaning is over now. Enjoy this day with your family members to celebrate successful completion of tiresome cleaning task.

Stay tuned for more wellness and cleanliness tips!

RECOMMENDED READING

UPCYCLING: Turning Trash To Treasure

smarturl.it/upcyclea

Creativity : Creative Thinking To Improve Memory, Increase Success and Live A Healthy Life

hyperurl.co/creative

MINIMALISTIC LIVING: How To Live In A Van and Get Off The Grid

hyperurl.co/offthegrid

SUGAR: Shut Your Mouth To Sugar Addiction And Cravings Forever

hyperurl.co/sugar

Made in the USA
Monee, IL
22 June 2024

60352739R00046